SOCCER LEGENDS ALPHABET

MEN

Words by Robin Feiner

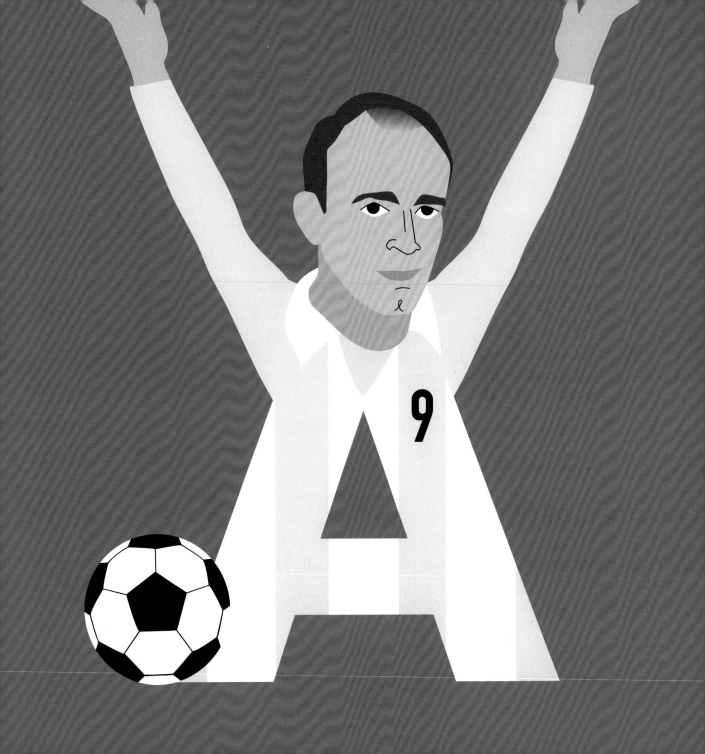

A is for **A**lfredo Di Stéfano. The 'Blond Arrow' was a visionary player who led Real Madrid to five consecutive European Cup titles, scoring in every final. Possessing endless stamina and an ability to play any position, it was said that with Di Stéfano in your side, "you had two players in every position!"

B is for Franz **B**eckenbauer. This versatile German legend is widely regarded as the greatest defender of all time, having revolutionized the modern sweeper role. A two-time European Footballer of the Year, 'Der Kaiser' is the only player to have won a World Cup as both captain and coach.

C is for Johan **C**ruyff.
A near-mythical figure, Cruyff revolutionized the modern game as a player and coach, popularizing 'Total Football' with Ajax, Barcelona and the Dutch national team. His creativity and dazzling skill, including his famed 'Cruyff turn,' have inspired generations of players.

D is for Alessandro **D**el Piero. This iconic Italian forward and Juventus legend awed opponents and fans alike with his on-field skill and off-field nobility. He won almost every major tournament at club and international level, and is the all-time leading scorer for his beloved Juve.

E is for **E**usébio.
The 'Black Panther' was
a gifted dribbler and lethal
striker who scored more than
a goal a game for both club
and country. With 11 league
titles, a European Cup and a
Ballon d'Or to his name, this
Portuguese legend even got
the better of Pelé, Di Stéfano
and Puskás in several
classic battles.

F is for **F**erenc Puskás. The 'Galloping Major' dazzled fans with his graceful form as a member of Hungary's 'Mighty Magyars' and as part of an unstoppable partnership with Di Stéfano at Real Madrid. Today, FIFA presents the Puskás Award to the player who scores the most beautiful goal of the year.

G is for **G**arrincha.
Born with a crooked spine and one leg shorter than the other, Garrincha was told by doctors that he'd be unable to play sports. But the 'Bent-Legged Angel' had the dribbling skills to make defenders look silly, delighting crowds who would chant 'olé' after each trick.

H is for Gheorghe Hagi. 'The Commander' blitzed his opponents with a rare blend of creativity and technical ability. Often referred to as the 'Maradona of the Carpathians,' Hagi was undeniably the greatest Romanian player of all time and one of the best footballers of his generation.

I is for Andrés **I**niesta. This once-in-a-generation central midfielder scored the winning goal in Spain's maiden 2010 World Cup victory. Known for his pinpoint passing and on-field intellect, 'The Illusionist' devoted 16 years of his career to Barcelona and is the most decorated Spanish footballer of all time.

J is for **Jürgen Klinsmann.**
**This German striker displayed
an admirable goal-scoring
prowess in a career that
included World Cup and Euro
titles. His 1994 transfer to
Tottenham – where he won
the hearts of hostile English
fans with good humor and a
memorable diving celebration
– paved the way for foreigners
in the Premier League.**

K is for Kenny Dalglish. Few players have needed as much space in their trophy cabinet as this Scottish legend. One of British soccer's most legendary goal scorers, Sir Kenny won 10 league titles, 10 domestic cups and three European Cups in his time with Celtic and Liverpool. To top it off, he won another four league titles as manager.

L is for Lionel Messi.
A creative genius and prolific finisher with a record seven Ballon d'Or awards, Messi holds the distinction of being the top goal scorer in Spanish La Liga history as well as a World Cup winner. Affectionately known as 'The Flea,' this pint-sized magician is the only player that runs faster with the ball than he does without it!

M is for Diego Maradona. Tiny in size but a giant on the field, 'The Golden Boy' possessed the perfect blend of speed, skill, maneuverability and power. Carving up entire teams with the ball seemingly attached to his foot, it is no surprise that Maradona was jointly named FIFA Player of the 20th Century alongside Pelé.

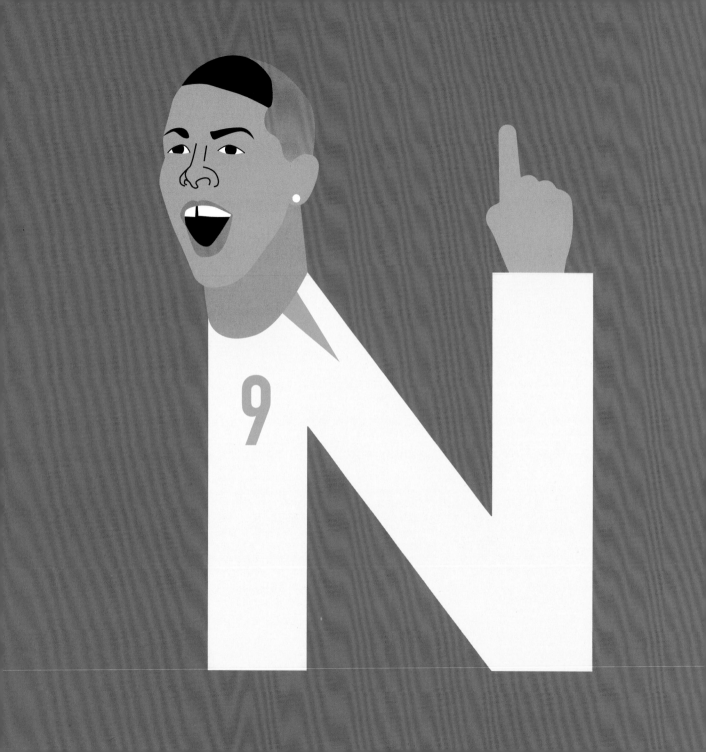

N is for Ronaldo Luís Nazário de Lima. One of the most naturally gifted footballers of all time, the 'original' Ronaldo dazzled fans with his ability to strike from any angle. The Brazilian master-mind could take on entire teams with a combination of flair, power and technique that the world had never seen before.

O is for Jay-Jay **O**kocha. Nigeria has never produced a better player than this attacking midfielder famously described as being "so good that they named him twice" – a line immortalized in chant by his Bolton fans. Thrilling spectators with his trickery and skill, Okocha inspired his country to Olympic gold in 1996.

P is for Pelé.
No name is more synonymous with soccer than 'Pelé.' The Brazilian forward for Santos boasts an astonishing resume that includes three World Cup trophies and the prestigious title of FIFA Player of the Century. He is hailed as a national hero for his contribution to 'The Beautiful Game' and his tireless charity work.

Q is for Ricardo **Q**uaresma. You don't earn the nickname 'The Magician' without blowing people away with feats of unbelievable skill. This Portuguese winger is so brilliant at the 'trivela' – curling the ball with the outside of his foot – that many think the move should be renamed the 'Quaresma.'

R is for Cristiano Ronaldo. No other player has transcended the game like 'CR7.' With five Ballon d'Or awards, one Euro Championship trophy and league titles in many different countries, Ronaldo is the all-time leading scorer for both Portugal and Real Madrid. Sii!

S is for Hugo Sánchez.
The pride of Mexico, this
goal-crazy forward for Real
Madrid fascinated fans and
critics alike with his acrobatic
finishes and trademark
somersault celebration.
With over 400 club goals
and another 29 for his country,
this legend is widely regarded
as the greatest Mexican
footballer of all time.

T is for **T**hierry Henry. This iconic French striker has won almost every possible trophy at club and national level. As the all-time leading goal scorer for both Arsenal and France, 'Titi' was the most effortless and composed finisher in Premier League history. Magnifique!

U is for **U**we Seeler.
Two decades as a striker
with Germany's Hamburger
SV solidified Seeler as a
legend, so much so that the
club immortalized him with
a giant statue of his right foot!
Ironically, his most famous
goal came on a sensational
backward header that
toppled England in the
1970 World Cup!

V is for Marco van Basten. With three Ballon d'Or awards by the age of 28, this Dutchman was a pure goal-scoring machine until an ankle injury forced his early retirement. His fabled volley brought home the Netherlands' one and only European Championship trophy in 1988. Legend!

Ww

W is for George **W**eah.
At his peak, 'King George' was unstoppable. With a rare combination of physical strength and unbelievable technical ability, Weah won three African Footballer of the Year awards and a Ballon d'Or. A legendary Liberian in more ways than one, Weah became the President of his home nation in 2015.

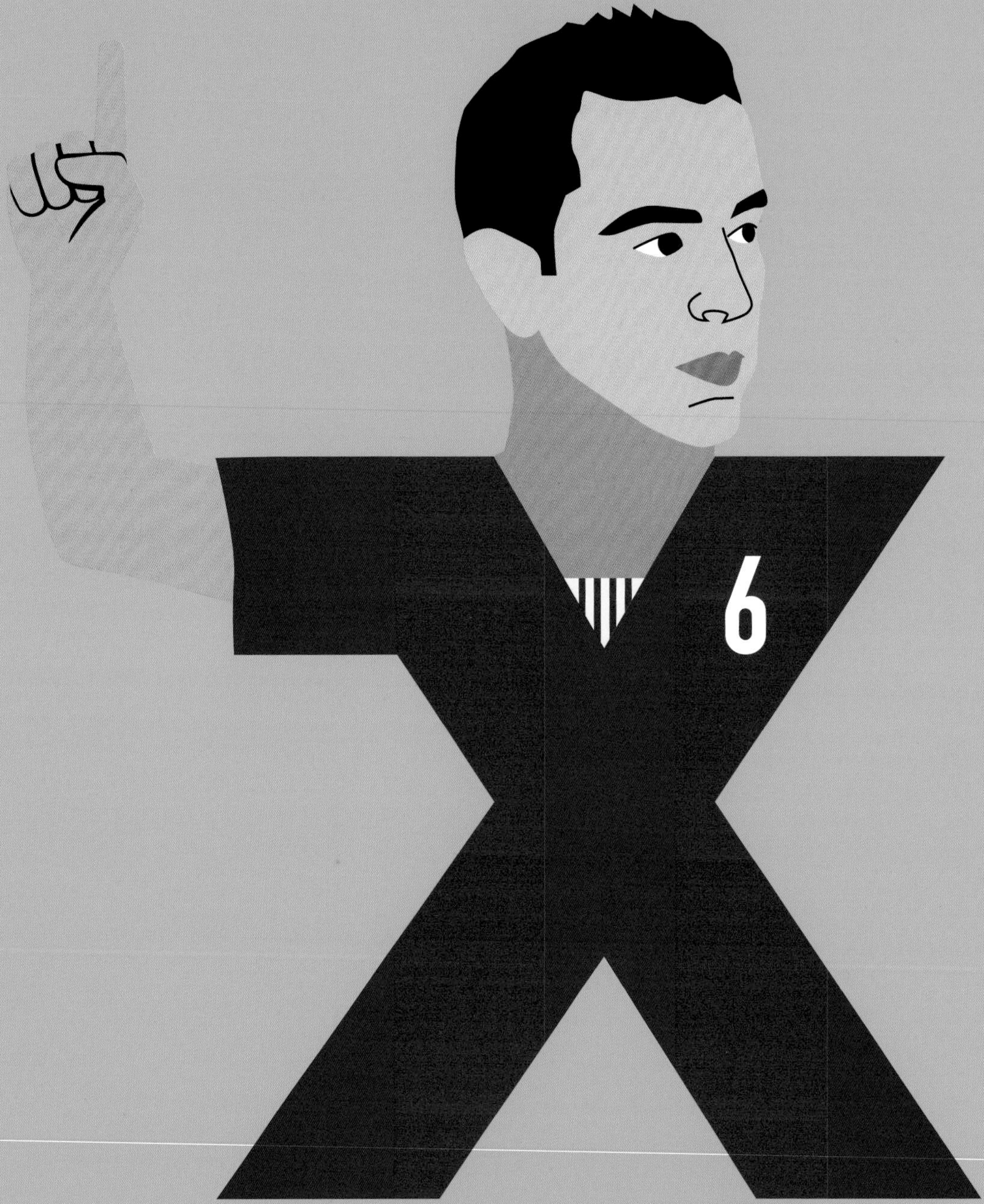
6

X is for **X**avi.
A Spanish institution and as humble as they come, the 'Puppet Master' took control of Barcelona with his ingenious playmaking ability and fluent 'tiki-taka' style of soccer.
As the heartbeat of Spain's midfield, Xavi helped his team to a 2010 World Cup victory.

CCCP

Y is for Lev Yashin. The 'Black Spider' was not only the best Russian footballer ever, but also the most iconic goalie ever. As a passionate and loyal member of Dynamo Moscow, Yashin dominated the 1950s and 60s with his pioneering style of coming off his line and controlling his team's entire defense.

Z is for Zinedine Zidane.
This highly decorated attacking midfielder from Juventus and Real Madrid holds a special place in French hearts, thanks to his cunning ability to '360 roulette' his way to classic victories. Doting peers have labeled 'Zizou' as "a monster from another planet" and "football's answer to the Bolshoi Ballet."

The ever-expanding legendary library

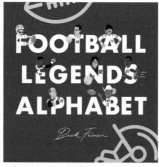

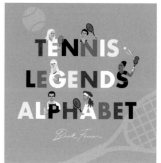

EXPLORE THESE LEGENDARY ALPHABETS & MORE AT WWW.ALPHABETLEGENDS.COM

SOCCER LEGENDS ALPHABET - MEN
www.alphabetlegends.com

Published by Alphabet Legends Pty Ltd in 2019
Created by Beck Feiner
Copyright © Alphabet Legends Pty Ltd 2019

9780648672418

ALPHABET LEGENDS